Burrowing Wisdom

Burrowing Wisdom

Matthew Petchinsky

Burrowing Wisdom: Life Lessons from the Groundhog
By: Matthew Petchinsky

Introduction: Exploring What We Can Learn from the Groundhog

The humble groundhog, also known as a woodchuck or whistle-pig, is more than just a curious mammal or the star of an annual February tradition. This small creature, deeply rooted in North American folklore and ecology, has a surprisingly profound connection to human life, the changing seasons, and our understanding of the natural world. By observing the groundhog's behaviors, habits, and symbolic significance, we can uncover lessons that resonate far beyond its burrow.

A Symbol of Seasonal Change

For many, the groundhog is synonymous with Groundhog Day, an event steeped in tradition and superstition. Each year on February 2nd, millions watch as this unassuming creature is called upon to predict the weather. Will winter persist, or is spring just around the corner? While this ritual is lighthearted, its origins reveal humanity's age-old desire to understand and predict nature's cycles. The groundhog's role as a harbinger of seasonal change reminds us of the importance of living in harmony with the rhythms of the Earth.

Seasonal awareness, symbolized by the groundhog, can teach us to be more attuned to the passage of time. The cycles of nature are mirrored in our lives—periods of growth, rest, reflection, and renewal. By studying how the groundhog interacts with its environment, we gain insight into how we, too, can adapt and thrive through life's seasons.

The Groundhog's Mastery of Preparation

Groundhogs are excellent planners. Their entire life cycle revolves around preparation and survival. In the summer and fall, they eat voraciously to build up body fat, ensuring they can endure their long hibernation. They meticulously construct their burrows, which are marvels of engineering, with designated chambers for sleeping, waste, and escape routes.

From the groundhog's industriousness, we can learn the value of foresight and preparation. Whether in our personal, professional, or spiritual lives, planning ahead ensures we can weather inevitable challenges. Groundhogs remind us that preparation is not just a chore—it is a survival skill and an investment in our future well-being.

The Power of Rest and Renewal

One of the most fascinating aspects of groundhog behavior is their hibernation. During the cold months, groundhogs enter a state of torpor, slowing their metabolism and conserving energy until spring arrives. This cycle of intense activity followed by deliberate rest offers a profound lesson: rest is not a sign of weakness but a necessary phase for growth and renewal.

In our fast-paced world, the groundhog's approach to hibernation encourages us to value rest. Taking the time to recharge, both physically and mentally, can enhance productivity and creativity. The groundhog's hibernation serves as a reminder that balance is essential, and periods of dormancy can lead to profound rejuvenation.

Adaptability and Resilience

Groundhogs are highly adaptable creatures. They thrive in diverse environments, from open fields to urban landscapes, demonstrating remarkable resilience in the face of change. Whether evading predators, surviving harsh winters, or adjusting to human encroachment, groundhogs embody the ability to adapt and overcome.

This resilience offers a powerful lesson for us. Life is full of uncertainties and challenges, but adaptability can turn obstacles into opportunities. The groundhog's ability to adjust and thrive is a testament to the strength found in flexibility and perseverance.

The Groundhog as a Spiritual Guide

In folklore and mythology, animals often serve as symbols or guides, offering wisdom and insight into the mysteries of life. The groundhog, with its deep connection to the Earth and the cycles of nature, represents introspection, transformation, and the emergence from darkness into light. Its journey from hibernation to the surface each spring mirrors our own spiritual journeys—periods of withdrawal and inner work followed by renewal and outward growth.

For those attuned to symbolism, the groundhog's burrow can be seen as a metaphor for the subconscious. Venturing into the burrow is akin to exploring our inner depths, confronting fears, and emerging with newfound understanding and clarity. In this way, the groundhog teaches us to embrace our inner shadows and find strength in self-discovery.

What We Stand to Gain

The lessons we can learn from the groundhog are as diverse as they are profound. Whether it's appreciating the cyclical nature of life, valuing the importance of rest and preparation, or learning to adapt and persevere, the groundhog offers a roadmap for living in harmony with ourselves and our environment. Beyond the folklore and festivities of Groundhog Day lies a deeper truth: the groundhog is not just a weather predictor but a wise teacher, embodying principles that resonate across cultures and ages.

As we explore the habits, behaviors, and symbolic meanings of this remarkable creature, let us take a moment to reflect on what the groundhog represents in our own lives. Perhaps, like the groundhog, we can emerge from our own winters—whether literal or metaphorical—and greet the coming spring with readiness, resilience, and hope.

Chapter 1: The Groundhog's Adaptability

Adaptability is one of the most vital traits for survival, both in the natural world and in human life. Few creatures exemplify this quality as well as the groundhog. Also known as the woodchuck, this small yet remarkable mammal has evolved to thrive in diverse environments, from dense forests and meadows to suburban backyards and even urban landscapes. In this chapter, we delve into the many ways the groundhog demonstrates adaptability, exploring its physical traits, behaviors, and survival strategies, and uncovering the lessons we can draw from its remarkable ability to adjust to a changing world.

Evolutionary Adaptations

The groundhog, a member of the marmot family, has evolved a variety of physical and behavioral traits that allow it to thrive in a wide range of habitats. These include:

- **Burrowing Mastery**: The groundhog's powerful forelimbs and long claws are perfectly adapted for digging complex burrow systems. These burrows are not just shelters but multifunctional structures that serve as homes, nurseries, and hibernation chambers. The groundhog's ability to adapt its burrow design to suit different soil types and environments is a testament to its ingenuity and flexibility.

- **Dietary Versatility**: Groundhogs are primarily herbivores, consuming a diet of grasses, wildflowers, fruits, and vegetables. However, they are opportunistic feeders, capable of adjusting their diet based on the availability of food in their environment. In agricultural areas, they may forage on crops, while in suburban settings, they can subsist on garden plants. This dietary flexibility ensures their survival even when food sources change.

- **Seasonal Adaptation**: Perhaps one of the most impressive aspects of the groundhog's adaptability is its ability to survive extreme seasonal changes. During the warmer months, groundhogs actively forage and build fat reserves. As winter approaches, they enter a state of hibernation, reducing their metabolic rate to conserve energy. This ability to adapt to seasonal cycles is a crucial survival strategy in temperate climates.

Behavioral Adaptability

Groundhogs are not only physically equipped for adaptation but also exhibit behaviors that allow them to navigate changing environments and threats.

- **Habitat Flexibility**: Groundhogs can make their homes in a variety of landscapes, from rural farmlands to the edges of bustling cities. They are adept at finding locations that offer both food and safety, such as areas near open fields with plenty of vegetation and access to shelter. This flexibility has enabled groundhogs to coexist with humans, even as their natural habitats shrink.

- **Defense Mechanisms**: While groundhogs are not aggressive by nature, they have developed several defense strategies to protect themselves from predators, including hawks, foxes, and coyotes. Their keen sense of hearing and sharp eyesight allow them to detect danger early. When threatened, they retreat to their burrows, which are designed with multiple entrances and escape routes. Groundhogs can also emit a high-pitched whistle to warn others of nearby danger, showcasing their ability to adapt communication for survival.

- **Reproductive Strategies**: Groundhogs adapt their reproductive behaviors to environmental conditions. In favorable conditions, they can produce larger litters, ensuring the continuation of their species. When resources are scarce, reproductive rates may decrease, demonstrating their ability to adjust to ecological pressures.

Adaptability in Urban Environments

One of the most fascinating examples of the groundhog's adaptability is its ability to thrive in urban and suburban environments. As human development encroaches on natural habitats, many species struggle to survive. Groundhogs, however, have found ways to coexist with humans. They often build burrows near gardens, under sheds, or along the edges of parks, taking advantage of the shelter and food provided by these spaces.

Urban groundhogs face unique challenges, such as increased encounters with humans and vehicles. Yet, they display remarkable resilience. They adjust their activity patterns to avoid humans, often becoming more active during early morning or late evening hours. This ability to alter their behavior based on their surroundings is a key aspect of their adaptability.

Lessons in Human Adaptability

The groundhog's ability to adjust and thrive in a changing world offers valuable lessons for humans. In many ways, we face challenges similar to those of the groundhog—changing environments, resource scarcity, and the need to navigate complex systems. By observing the groundhog's adaptability, we can learn to:

- **Embrace Change**: Change is inevitable, but adaptability allows us to face it with resilience. The groundhog's ability to adjust its behavior, diet, and habitat to suit its surroundings reminds us of the importance of flexibility in overcoming life's challenges.
- **Build Strong Foundations**: Just as the groundhog constructs secure and multifunctional burrows, we can create strong foundations in our lives—whether through financial stability, supportive relationships, or personal growth—that enable us to weather storms and adapt to new circumstances.
- **Stay Resourceful**: The groundhog's dietary and behavioral flexibility illustrates the importance of resourcefulness. By being open to new opportunities and solutions, we can navigate even the most unexpected challenges.
- **Balance Activity and Rest**: Groundhogs are masters of balance, alternating between periods of intense activity and rest. This serves as a reminder of the need to balance productivity with self-care in our own lives.

The Groundhog as a Model of Resilience

In a rapidly changing world, the groundhog's adaptability serves as an inspiring example of resilience. Its ability to thrive in diverse environments, adjust to seasonal cycles, and navigate the challenges of co-existence with humans is a testament to the power of flexibility and resourcefulness. Whether in nature or in life, adaptability is the key to survival and success.

As we move forward, let us take a moment to reflect on the groundhog's quiet yet profound example. By embracing adaptability, we can not only survive but also thrive, finding opportunities for growth and renewal in the face of change. The groundhog, in its unassuming way, reminds us that resilience is not just about enduring—it's about evolving.

Chapter 2: Surviving Winter: Lessons on Resilience

Winter is a time of scarcity, cold, and challenge, and for the groundhog, it is a critical test of survival. While many animals migrate or remain active throughout the year, groundhogs employ a unique and highly effective strategy to weather the harsh winter months: hibernation. This remarkable adaptation not only ensures their survival but also offers valuable lessons on resilience that we can apply to our own lives. In this chapter, we explore the groundhog's approach to surviving winter, from its meticulous preparation to the biological marvel of hibernation, and uncover the profound insights these strategies provide.

The Art of Preparation: Building Resilience Before the Storm

Groundhogs begin their winter survival journey long before the first frost. Preparation is the cornerstone of their strategy, emphasizing the importance of foresight and planning.

- **Fat Reserves as Life Insurance**: During the warmer months, groundhogs consume vast amounts of food to build up body fat. These fat reserves serve as their primary energy source during hibernation, ensuring they can survive months without eating. This preparatory phase highlights the importance of saving resources during times of abundance to sustain us through periods of scarcity.

- **Burrow Engineering**: The groundhog's burrow is an engineering marvel, designed with resilience in mind. These burrows are multi-chambered, with separate areas for sleeping, waste, and escape routes. Burrows are dug deep enough to remain insulated against the cold, providing a safe refuge during winter. This level of preparation underscores the importance of creating secure, multifunctional spaces in our own lives—whether physical, financial, or emotional—to protect against unforeseen challenges.

The Biology of Resilience: Understanding Hibernation

Hibernation is the groundhog's ultimate survival tool, a biological adaptation that allows it to endure even the harshest winters. The process involves a dramatic reduction in metabolic activity, conserving energy when resources are scarce.

- **Metabolic Slowdown**: During hibernation, a groundhog's heart rate drops from 80-100 beats per minute to as few as 5 beats per minute. Their body temperature falls from around 99°F (37°C) to as low as 38°F (3°C). These changes drastically reduce energy expenditure, allowing them to survive on their fat reserves.
- **Energy Conservation**: The ability to slow their metabolism is a masterclass in resource management. Groundhogs teach us that resilience isn't just about working harder but working smarter. In times of challenge, conserving energy and focusing on essential priorities can help us navigate difficulties without burning out.
- **Periodic Arousal**: Even during hibernation, groundhogs occasionally wake to adjust their position or move within the burrow. This periodic activity prevents stiffness and ensures their survival until spring. Similarly, we must remain adaptable and responsive even during periods of rest or inactivity, staying prepared for any changes in our environment.

Facing Challenges: Coping with the Unexpected

Winter is unpredictable, and despite their meticulous preparation, groundhogs sometimes face unforeseen challenges. These situations demonstrate their ability to adapt and persevere.

- **Predators and Disturbances**: Even in the depths of hibernation, groundhogs are vulnerable to predators that may dig into their burrows. Their strategy of building multiple entrances and exits allows them to escape if threatened. This highlights the importance of having contingency plans in our own lives.
- **Changing Climates**: As winters become less predictable due to climate change, groundhogs must adjust their hibernation patterns. Some studies suggest that groundhogs are waking earlier from hibernation, a potential survival risk if food is not yet available. This adaptability underscores the need for flexibility and resilience in the face of changing circumstances.

Lessons from the Groundhog: Building Human Resilience

The groundhog's strategies for surviving winter offer profound lessons that can help us cultivate resilience in our own lives:

- **Prepare in Times of Plenty**: Just as groundhogs build fat reserves and burrows, we can create our own "reserves" during good times. This might involve saving money, building supportive relationships, or learning new skills that will help us during tougher periods.
- **Create Safe Spaces**: A well-designed burrow is essential for a groundhog's survival. In our own lives, creating safe and nurturing spaces—whether physical homes or emotional sanctuaries—can provide us with the refuge we need during challenging times.
- **Conserve Energy Wisely**: Hibernation teaches us the value of energy management. During times of stress or scarcity, it's important to focus on what truly matters and let go of nonessential tasks or distractions.
- **Adapt to Change**: Winter is rarely predictable, and resilience often comes from our ability to adapt. Whether it's adjusting to a new job, dealing with unexpected challenges, or navigating personal loss, flexibility is key to surviving and thriving.
- **Rest is Essential**: Hibernation is a reminder that rest is not a luxury but a necessity. Taking time to recharge, whether through sleep, meditation, or relaxation, is crucial for maintaining resilience and avoiding burnout.

The Symbolism of Winter: Growth in the Darkness

Winter, with its cold and barren landscapes, is often seen as a metaphor for life's challenges. However, it is also a season of growth and transformation. Beneath the snow-covered ground, seeds lie dormant, waiting for spring. In the same way, the groundhog's hibernation is not merely a pause but a preparation for renewal.

For humans, winter can represent periods of introspection and self-discovery. Just as the groundhog retreats to its burrow, we, too, can use challenging times to turn inward, reflect, and prepare for new beginnings. This perspective encourages us to view hardships not as endpoints but as opportunities for growth.

Emerging Stronger: The Groundhog's Springtime Revival

When winter ends and spring begins, groundhogs emerge from their burrows, leaner but alive. They immediately resume their activities, foraging and preparing for the next cycle of seasons. This resilience, honed through months of preparation and adaptation, is a powerful testament to the groundhog's survival instincts.

Similarly, when we face and overcome challenges, we emerge stronger, more resourceful, and better prepared for the future. The groundhog's revival each spring serves as a reminder that resilience is not just about surviving—it's about thriving after adversity.

Conclusion: A Guide for Human Resilience

The groundhog's approach to surviving winter is a masterclass in resilience. Through preparation, adaptability, energy conservation, and rest, these small creatures navigate one of nature's harshest seasons with grace and efficiency. For humans, these lessons can be transformative.

By adopting the groundhog's strategies in our own lives, we can better navigate life's winters—those inevitable periods of difficulty, scarcity, and challenge. Like the groundhog, we can prepare, adapt, and rest, emerging stronger and more resilient when spring finally arrives.

Chapter 3: Emerging from the Burrow: Embracing Change

Emerging from the burrow after a long, dormant winter is a defining moment for the groundhog. It is an act of renewal, courage, and adaptation, symbolizing the beginning of a new season and the acceptance of inevitable change. For humans, stepping out of our metaphorical burrows—our comfort zones, routines, or periods of stagnation—can be equally challenging and transformative. This chapter explores the groundhog's process of re-entering the world after hibernation and uncovers lessons we can apply to our own lives about embracing change, overcoming fear, and thriving in new circumstances.

The Transition from Dormancy to Activity

Emerging from hibernation is no small feat for the groundhog. After months of inactivity, their bodies must readjust to movement, foraging, and social interactions. This transition mirrors the challenges humans face when moving from a period of rest or stagnation to one of growth and action.

- **Reawakening the Body**: A groundhog's body must gradually recover from its slowed metabolism and reduced muscle tone. Similarly, humans often need time to adjust after periods of inactivity, whether physical, emotional, or mental. This process reminds us to approach transitions with patience and care, allowing time for re-adaptation.

- **Reestablishing Routines**: Once awake, the groundhog's first priority is survival. They begin foraging to replenish their depleted energy reserves and prepare for the demands of spring. This return to routine highlights the importance of grounding ourselves in productive habits as we navigate change.

- **Exploring the Environment**: The world outside the burrow is rarely the same as when the groundhog entered it. Snow may have melted, predators may be lurking, and food sources may have shifted. Groundhogs instinctively adapt to these changes, teaching us the value of curiosity and flexibility when encountering new circumstances.

Overcoming the Fear of the Unknown

For a groundhog, emerging from the burrow is inherently risky. Predators, harsh weather, or a lack of food can make this transition fraught with danger. Yet, they instinctively know that remaining underground is not an option. This willingness to face uncertainty offers profound lessons for humans.

- **The Necessity of Change**: Staying in the burrow may feel safe, but it is unsustainable. Without food or sunlight, the groundhog would eventually weaken. Similarly, humans often resist change out of fear or comfort, but stagnation can prevent growth and lead to missed opportunities. Embracing change is not just a choice—it's a necessity for survival and progress.
- **Courage in the Face of Fear**: The groundhog's cautious yet determined emergence from its burrow demonstrates the importance of balancing prudence with bravery. For humans, this means acknowledging our fears while taking deliberate steps toward the unknown. True courage is not the absence of fear but the willingness to act despite it.
- **Learning Through Exploration**: The groundhog's first steps out of the burrow are exploratory, assessing the environment for safety and opportunity. This approach teaches us to embrace change as a learning experience, gathering information and adjusting our actions as we go.

Adapting to a New Season

Spring brings not only opportunities but also challenges. The groundhog's ability to adapt to these changes is a testament to its resilience and resourcefulness.

- **Renewing Energy**: After months of dormancy, the groundhog focuses on rebuilding its strength by foraging for nutrient-rich food. For humans, emerging from a period of change requires similar replenishment, whether it's physical energy, emotional support, or intellectual growth. Investing in self-care and renewal is essential for thriving in new circumstances.
- **Seizing Opportunities**: Spring is a time of abundance, but it is fleeting. Groundhogs work diligently to capitalize on the season's resources, preparing for the future. This proactive mindset reminds us to take advantage of opportunities as they arise, recognizing that they may not last forever.
- **Navigating Challenges**: Even in spring, groundhogs face predators, unpredictable weather, and competition for resources. Their ability to navigate these challenges underscores the importance of adaptability and resilience in the face of adversity.

The Groundhog as a Metaphor for Personal Growth

The groundhog's emergence from its burrow is a powerful metaphor for personal growth and transformation. Just as the groundhog leaves its safe haven to embrace a new season, we, too, must step out of our comfort zones to grow and evolve.

- **The Cycles of Life**: The groundhog's journey reflects the cyclical nature of life—periods of rest and activity, preparation and action, dormancy and renewal. Recognizing and respecting these cycles can help us navigate change with greater ease and confidence.
- **The Power of Small Steps**: The groundhog does not sprint out of its burrow without assessing its surroundings. Instead, it takes small, deliberate steps. This approach teaches us that even the most significant changes can be managed through incremental progress.
- **Transformation Through Action**: By leaving the burrow, the groundhog transforms from a dormant creature to an active participant in its ecosystem. Similarly, taking action, no matter how small, can transform our lives and help us adapt to new realities.

Embracing Change in Human Life

The lessons we learn from the groundhog's emergence can be applied to many aspects of human life, from personal growth to professional transitions and societal shifts.

- **Acknowledge the Need for Change**: Recognize when staying in your comfort zone is no longer serving you. Just as the groundhog cannot remain underground indefinitely, we must accept that change is a natural and necessary part of life.
- **Prepare for Transitions**: Like the groundhog building fat reserves and a sturdy burrow, preparation can ease the challenges of change. Whether it's learning new skills, saving resources, or building a support network, preparation provides a foundation for success.
- **Face Uncertainty with Confidence**: Change often brings uncertainty, but the groundhog's willingness to explore its new environment teaches us that curiosity and courage can help us navigate the unknown.
- **Adapt to New Realities**: Be flexible and open-minded as you encounter new challenges and opportunities. The groundhog's ability to adjust its behavior based on its environment reminds us that adaptability is key to thriving in a changing world.
- **Celebrate Renewal**: Embrace change as an opportunity for growth and renewal. Just as the groundhog emerges to a new season full of possibilities, we, too, can view change as a chance to start fresh and pursue new goals.

Conclusion: Thriving in the Light of Change

Emerging from the burrow is not just an act of survival for the groundhog—it is a declaration of resilience, courage, and adaptability. For humans, embracing change requires similar qualities, as well as a willingness to learn, grow, and take risks. By observing the groundhog's journey, we can find inspiration and guidance for navigating our own transitions and stepping into the light of new opportunities.

Change is not always easy, but it is essential for growth. Like the groundhog, we must venture out of our burrows, face the challenges and opportunities of a new season, and embrace the possibilities that lie ahead. In doing so, we can transform our lives, one small step at a time.

Chapter 4: Living in Harmony with Nature

Nature is a profound teacher, offering countless lessons on balance, resilience, and interconnectivity. Among its many inhabitants, the groundhog exemplifies the principles of living in harmony with the environment. Through its behaviors, diet, and interactions with its ecosystem, the groundhog demonstrates a sustainable way of life that is deeply attuned to the rhythms of the natural world. This chapter explores how the groundhog lives symbiotically with its surroundings and what we can learn from its practices to foster harmony in our own relationship with nature.

The Groundhog's Place in the Ecosystem

Groundhogs, as burrowing mammals, play a vital role in their ecosystems. Their behaviors contribute to soil health, biodiversity, and the well-being of other species.

- **Soil Aeration and Fertility**: By digging extensive burrows, groundhogs aerate the soil, allowing oxygen and water to penetrate deeper layers. This process improves soil health and promotes plant growth. Additionally, groundhog burrows redistribute nutrients, enriching the soil over time.

- **Supporting Biodiversity**: Groundhog burrows often become habitats for other species, such as foxes, rabbits, snakes, and insects, after they are abandoned. This creates micro-ecosystems that support a wide variety of life. The groundhog's ability to share its resources highlights the interconnectedness of all living things.

- **Predator-Prey Relationships**: Groundhogs are prey for many predators, including hawks, coyotes, and foxes. Their presence in the food chain sustains higher predators, contributing to a balanced ecosystem. This dynamic illustrates the importance of every species, no matter its size, in maintaining ecological balance.

The Groundhog's Sustainable Lifestyle

The groundhog's way of life is inherently sustainable, driven by its needs rather than excess. Its behaviors and habits offer valuable lessons in living lightly on the Earth.

- **Minimal Resource Use**: Groundhogs consume only what they need to survive, primarily feeding on a plant-based diet of grasses, fruits, and vegetables. This restrained consumption aligns with the principles of sustainability, emphasizing the importance of taking only what is necessary.
- **Natural Resource Recycling**: Groundhog burrows are reused and repurposed by other animals, ensuring that no resource is wasted. This recycling of habitat teaches us to find new uses for existing resources, reducing waste and promoting sustainability.
- **Seasonal Living**: The groundhog adapts its lifestyle to the seasons, hibernating during winter when food is scarce and actively foraging during spring and summer. This cyclical living reflects an understanding of nature's rhythms and the value of adjusting one's behavior to match environmental conditions.

Lessons from the Groundhog: Building a Harmonious Relationship with Nature

The groundhog's interaction with its environment offers profound insights into how humans can live more sustainably and harmoniously with the natural world.

- **Respect for Cycles**: Nature operates in cycles—day and night, seasons, life and death. The groundhog's ability to adapt to these cycles teaches us to respect and align our actions with nature's rhythms. For example, planting crops in season and conserving energy during colder months are ways to honor these cycles.
- **Coexisting with Other Species**: Groundhogs do not dominate their environment; they coexist with other species. Humans, too, must strive for coexistence, recognizing that our actions impact countless other forms of life.
- **Simplicity in Living**: The groundhog's life is one of simplicity, focused on meeting basic needs and avoiding excess. Adopting a minimalist mindset—reducing consumption and waste—can help us live more harmoniously with nature.
- **Conservation of Resources**: Groundhogs instinctively conserve energy and resources, whether by hibernating in winter or eating selectively. Humans can follow suit by practicing energy conservation, using renewable resources, and reducing our ecological footprint.

Connecting with Nature Through Observation

The groundhog's harmonious relationship with nature is rooted in its deep connection to the environment. By observing and understanding nature, humans can foster a similar connection.

- **The Power of Observation**: Groundhogs are highly attuned to their surroundings, constantly observing for predators, food sources, and environmental changes. For humans, taking time to observe nature—whether through hiking, gardening, or simply watching wildlife—can deepen our understanding and appreciation of the natural world.
- **Learning from Ecosystems**: Nature operates as an interconnected web, with each species playing a role. By studying ecosystems, we can learn how to create systems in our own lives that are sustainable and self-regulating, such as permaculture gardening or zero-waste living.
- **Mindfulness in Nature**: Spending time in natural settings fosters mindfulness and a sense of peace. Like the groundhog, which instinctively aligns its actions with its environment, we can use nature as a guide for living in balance and harmony.

Challenges to Harmony: Human Impact on Groundhogs

While groundhogs live in harmony with nature, human activities often disrupt this balance, posing challenges to their survival.

- **Habitat Destruction**: Urbanization and agriculture reduce the groundhog's natural habitats, forcing them to adapt to human-dominated environments. This highlights the need for sustainable land use and conservation efforts.
- **Conflict with Humans**: Groundhogs are sometimes seen as pests, particularly when they burrow near gardens or agricultural fields. Understanding their ecological role and implementing non-lethal deterrents can help mitigate conflicts and foster coexistence.
- **Climate Change**: Changing weather patterns affect the groundhog's hibernation cycles and food availability. Addressing climate change through sustainable practices and policies is essential for protecting not only groundhogs but all species.

Taking Action: How Humans Can Live in Harmony with Nature

The groundhog's sustainable lifestyle provides a roadmap for humans to follow. By adopting practices that mirror the groundhog's harmony with the environment, we can create a more balanced and sustainable world.

- **Support Biodiversity**: Create habitats that support a variety of species, such as planting native plants, building wildlife corridors, and protecting natural areas.
- **Reduce Waste**: Practice the "three R's"—reduce, reuse, recycle—to minimize your impact on the environment. Emulate the groundhog's efficient use of resources by finding ways to repurpose and conserve.
- **Live Seasonally**: Align your lifestyle with the seasons, such as eating seasonal foods, conserving energy in winter, and spending more time outdoors in summer. Seasonal living reduces strain on natural resources and enhances your connection to nature.
- **Advocate for Conservation**: Support policies and organizations that protect habitats and promote sustainable practices. By protecting species like the groundhog, we preserve the intricate web of life that sustains all creatures.

Conclusion: A Blueprint for Balance

Living in harmony with nature is not merely a goal—it is a necessity for the health and survival of all life on Earth. The groundhog's behaviors and interactions with its environment offer a powerful model of sustainability, balance, and respect for nature's rhythms.

By observing and emulating the groundhog's practices, we can foster a deeper connection with the natural world and learn to live in a way that benefits both ourselves and the planet. In doing so, we honor the wisdom of nature and take a meaningful step toward a more harmonious and sustainable future. Like the groundhog, we, too, can become stewards of the Earth, living not in opposition to nature but as part of its intricate and beautiful design.

Chapter 5: Applying Groundhog Wisdom to Modern Life

The groundhog's way of life offers a treasure trove of wisdom for navigating modern challenges. From its meticulous preparation and harmonious relationship with nature to its adaptability and resilience, the groundhog embodies principles that humans can emulate in their own lives. In this chapter, we will delve into how the behaviors and survival strategies of the groundhog can be translated into actionable insights for living a more balanced, purposeful, and resilient life in today's fast-paced world.

Lesson 1: The Power of Preparation

Groundhogs are masters of preparation. Their survival during harsh winters depends on the careful accumulation of resources, strategic burrow building, and energy conservation. In modern life, preparation is equally essential, whether for career success, financial stability, or personal growth.

- **Strategic Planning**: Like the groundhog building its burrow, humans can benefit from creating structured plans for their goals. This might include setting clear objectives, breaking them into manageable steps, and identifying potential obstacles in advance.
- **Emergency Readiness**: The groundhog's fat reserves are a biological emergency fund. In human terms, building financial savings, maintaining emergency supplies, or preparing for unexpected life events can provide security and peace of mind.
- **Long-Term Thinking**: Groundhogs prepare not just for the immediate future but for the long winter ahead. Similarly, adopting a long-term perspective when making decisions—whether investing, learning new skills, or nurturing relationships—ensures that short-term actions align with long-term goals.

Lesson 2: The Balance Between Activity and Rest

The groundhog's life alternates between intense activity in the warmer months and deep rest during hibernation. This natural rhythm teaches us the importance of balance—a lesson often overlooked in our hyper-connected, productivity-driven culture.

- **Avoiding Burnout**: Groundhogs hibernate to conserve energy, recognizing the value of rest. In our own lives, prioritizing rest and recovery—through proper sleep, relaxation, or mindfulness practices—can enhance productivity and well-being.
- **Seasonal Living**: Just as groundhogs adjust their activities based on the season, humans can benefit from syncing their lives with seasonal cycles. This might mean focusing on outdoor activities and growth in spring and summer, while using fall and winter for reflection and planning.
- **Mindful Scheduling**: Groundhogs do not expend energy unnecessarily. Similarly, adopting a mindful approach to scheduling—focusing on high-priority tasks and avoiding overcommitment—can create a more sustainable work-life balance.

Lesson 3: Adapting to Change

Groundhogs thrive in diverse environments and respond to changing conditions with remarkable flexibility. In a world where change is constant, adaptability is a critical skill for success and resilience.

- **Embracing Uncertainty**: The groundhog faces unpredictable challenges, from weather fluctuations to predator threats. In modern life, embracing uncertainty and viewing change as an opportunity for growth can foster resilience.
- **Continuous Learning**: Adaptation often requires learning new skills or approaches. Whether it's staying updated on industry trends, developing technological fluency, or acquiring knowledge in a new field, a commitment to lifelong learning mirrors the groundhog's instinctive ability to adjust.
- **Resilience in Setbacks**: The groundhog's escape routes in its burrow reflect its preparedness for setbacks. In our lives, building resilience through strong support systems, contingency plans, and a positive mindset ensures we can recover and thrive when challenges arise.

Lesson 4: Living Sustainably

Groundhogs live lightly on the Earth, consuming only what they need and leaving a minimal footprint on their environment. In contrast, modern lifestyles often strain natural resources. The groundhog's sustainable practices provide a model for mindful consumption.

- **Minimalism and Moderation**: Groundhogs' simple lives remind us to focus on essentials rather than excess. Practicing minimalism—whether by decluttering, reducing waste, or prioritizing quality over quantity—can lead to greater fulfillment and environmental benefits.
- **Mindful Resource Use**: Like the groundhog conserving energy during hibernation, humans can adopt practices such as energy efficiency, water conservation, and recycling to reduce their ecological impact.
- **Support for Biodiversity**: By recognizing our role in the ecosystem, we can contribute to environmental health. Planting native species, creating wildlife habitats, and reducing pesticide use are just a few ways to live harmoniously with nature.

Lesson 5: Strength in Community

Although groundhogs are solitary creatures, their burrows often support other species, contributing to the ecosystem's overall health. This quiet generosity reflects the importance of community and collaboration in human life.

- **Building Networks**: Just as the groundhog's burrow benefits multiple species, humans thrive through strong networks of family, friends, and colleagues. Investing in relationships and helping others creates a ripple effect of support and well-being.
- **Mutual Aid**: The groundhog's role in its ecosystem highlights the value of contributing to the greater good. Volunteering, mentoring, or supporting community initiatives fosters a sense of purpose and connection.
- **Learning from Others**: While the groundhog adapts to its environment independently, it also benefits indirectly from the activities of other species. Humans can similarly grow by learning from diverse perspectives and experiences.

Lesson 6: Courage to Step Out of Comfort Zones

Emerging from its burrow after hibernation is a brave act for the groundhog, requiring it to face predators and unknown challenges. This courage serves as a metaphor for stepping out of comfort zones in human life.

- **Pursuing Growth**: Growth often requires leaving behind familiar routines and embracing new experiences. Whether it's pursuing a new career, starting a creative project, or traveling to unfamiliar places, taking risks can lead to personal transformation.
- **Facing Fear**: Like the groundhog cautiously assessing its surroundings, humans can face fears incrementally. Breaking down intimidating tasks into smaller steps makes them more manageable and less overwhelming.
- **Reinvention Through Change**: The groundhog's emergence signals a new season and a fresh start. Similarly, embracing change as an opportunity for reinvention allows us to align our lives with our evolving goals and values.

Lesson 7: Reflection and Self-Awareness

Groundhogs are attuned to their environment, responding to subtle changes in temperature, light, and food availability. This sensitivity reflects the importance of self-awareness and reflection in human life.

- **Listening to Inner Signals**: Just as the groundhog senses when it's time to hibernate or emerge, humans benefit from paying attention to their physical, emotional, and mental states. Practices like journaling, meditation, or therapy can enhance self-awareness.
- **Periodic Reflection**: The groundhog's hibernation period can be seen as a time of reflection and renewal. Setting aside time for introspection—whether through retreats, quiet time, or goal-setting sessions—helps clarify priorities and fosters personal growth.
- **Aligning with Natural Rhythms**: By observing and honoring natural cycles, we can align our actions with what feels most natural and sustainable, reducing stress and enhancing productivity.

Practical Applications: Groundhog Wisdom in Everyday Life

To apply the groundhog's lessons in modern life, consider the following actionable strategies:

1. **Plan Ahead**: Create a financial safety net, prepare for career transitions, and build skills that anticipate future needs.
2. **Prioritize Rest**: Schedule regular breaks, prioritize sleep, and engage in activities that rejuvenate your energy.
3. **Adapt Gracefully**: View challenges as opportunities to learn and grow, and approach change with curiosity rather than resistance.
4. **Live Lightly**: Reduce consumption, minimize waste, and practice gratitude for what you have.
5. **Foster Connections**: Build a strong support system and actively contribute to your community's well-being.
6. **Take Risks**: Step out of your comfort zone to pursue meaningful goals and experiences.
7. **Reflect Regularly**: Make time for self-assessment, goal evaluation, and mindfulness practices.

Conclusion: Groundhog Wisdom for a Meaningful Life

The groundhog's life may seem simple, but it is rich with lessons that resonate deeply with the complexities of human existence. By observing and applying its wisdom, we can cultivate resilience, embrace change, and live in greater harmony with ourselves, our communities, and the natural world.

In the end, the groundhog reminds us that life is a journey of preparation, adaptation, and renewal. By following its example, we can navigate modern challenges with purpose and grace, emerging stronger and more fulfilled with each season of life.

Appendix A: Resilience and Adaptation Strategies

Resilience and adaptation are essential traits for navigating life's challenges and thriving in an ever-changing world. Drawing inspiration from the groundhog's ability to prepare, endure, and adjust, this appendix provides practical strategies and insights to help you build resilience and embrace adaptation in your personal, professional, and emotional life.

Section 1: Building Personal Resilience

Personal resilience is the ability to recover from setbacks, face adversity, and grow stronger through challenges. It involves mental toughness, emotional flexibility, and a commitment to self-care.

1. Develop a Growth Mindset

- **Definition**: A growth mindset is the belief that abilities and intelligence can be developed through effort and learning.
- **How to Practice**:
    - Reframe challenges as opportunities for growth.
    - Focus on the process of learning rather than the outcome.
    - Celebrate progress, no matter how small.

2. Cultivate Emotional Regulation

- **Definition**: Emotional regulation is the ability to manage and respond to emotions in a healthy way.
- **How to Practice**:
    - Use mindfulness techniques, such as deep breathing or meditation, to stay grounded.
    - Recognize and label emotions to reduce their intensity.
    - Develop healthy outlets for stress, such as journaling, exercise, or creative activities.

3. Build a Support System

- **Definition**: A network of relationships that provides emotional, practical, and psychological support.
- **How to Practice**:
    - Surround yourself with positive and supportive individuals.
    - Seek mentors or join groups that align with your goals and interests.
    - Offer support to others to strengthen mutual connections.

4. Strengthen Problem-Solving Skills

- **Definition**: The ability to find effective solutions to challenges.
- **How to Practice**:
    - Break problems into smaller, manageable parts.
    - Brainstorm multiple solutions and evaluate their pros and cons.
    - Stay flexible and adjust strategies as needed.

5. Practice Self-Care

- **Definition**: Intentional activities that promote physical, emotional, and mental well-being.
- **How to Practice**:
    - Prioritize sleep, nutrition, and exercise.
    - Set boundaries to protect your time and energy.
    - Engage in activities that bring joy and relaxation.

Section 2: Adapting to Change

Adaptation is the process of adjusting to new circumstances, environments, or challenges. It requires flexibility, creativity, and a willingness to embrace the unknown.

1. Embrace Uncertainty

- **Definition**: Accepting that not all aspects of life can be controlled or predicted.
- **How to Practice**:
    - Focus on what you can control, such as your attitude and actions.
    - Let go of the need for perfection or complete certainty.
    - Practice gratitude for the present moment.

2. Stay Open to Learning

- **Definition**: A willingness to acquire new knowledge and skills to adapt to changing circumstances.
- **How to Practice**:
    - Seek out opportunities for professional development or personal growth.
    - Stay curious and ask questions to expand your understanding.
    - View mistakes as valuable lessons rather than failures.

3. Maintain Flexibility

- **Definition**: The ability to adjust goals, plans, and behaviors in response to change.
- **How to Practice**:
    - Set realistic expectations and remain open to alternative outcomes.
    - Use setbacks as a chance to reevaluate and refine your approach.
    - Balance long-term goals with short-term adjustments.

4. Build Cognitive Flexibility

- **Definition**: The ability to shift thinking and see situations from multiple perspectives.
- **How to Practice**:
    - Challenge your assumptions and consider alternative viewpoints.
    - Engage in activities that stimulate creativity, such as brainstorming or problem-solving games.
    - Practice adaptability in daily life by trying new routines or exploring unfamiliar ideas.

5. Develop Resourcefulness

- **Definition**: The ability to find innovative solutions and make the most of available resources.
- **How to Practice**:
    - Use constraints as an opportunity to think creatively.
    - Leverage your existing skills and tools in new ways.
    - Seek out partnerships or collaborations to amplify your efforts.

Section 3: Resilience Strategies for Specific Life Areas

Resilience and adaptation can be applied to various aspects of life, including work, relationships, and personal development. Below are tailored strategies for common challenges.

1. Professional Resilience

- **Navigate Workplace Change**:
    - Stay informed about industry trends and technological advancements.
    - Build a diverse skill set to increase job security and marketability.
- **Handle Job Stress**:
    - Use time management techniques, such as prioritizing tasks and delegating when possible.
    - Take regular breaks to avoid burnout.
- **Pursue Career Growth**:
    - Set clear professional goals and take proactive steps to achieve them.
    - Seek feedback and use it to improve your performance.

2. Relationship Resilience

- **Improve Communication**:
    - Practice active listening to understand others' perspectives.
    - Express thoughts and feelings honestly but respectfully.
- **Resolve Conflicts**:
    - Focus on finding solutions rather than assigning blame.
    - Be willing to compromise and collaborate for mutual benefit.
- **Strengthen Bonds**:
    - Spend quality time with loved ones and prioritize meaningful connections.
    - Show appreciation and gratitude for the people in your life.

3. Personal Growth Resilience

- **Set and Pursue Goals**:
    - Break long-term goals into smaller, actionable steps.
    - Celebrate milestones to stay motivated.
- **Develop Healthy Habits**:
    - Establish routines that support your physical and mental well-being.
    - Use positive reinforcement to maintain consistency.
- **Overcome Setbacks**:
    - Reflect on challenges to identify lessons and opportunities for growth.
    - Focus on progress rather than perfection.

Section 4: Tools and Resources for Resilience and Adaptation

To further enhance your resilience and adaptability, consider using the following tools and practices:

1. Journaling

- Keep a resilience journal to track challenges, solutions, and personal growth.
- Reflect on what worked well and what can be improved.

2. Mindfulness and Meditation

- Practice mindfulness to stay present and reduce stress.
- Use guided meditations focused on resilience and adaptation.

3. Visualization

- Imagine yourself successfully navigating challenges and achieving goals.
- Use visualization to build confidence and clarity.

4. Support Groups

- Join groups or communities that align with your interests and goals.
- Share experiences and learn from others facing similar challenges.

5. Educational Resources

- Read books, attend workshops, or take online courses on resilience and adaptability.
- Seek out role models or mentors who exemplify these qualities.

Conclusion: Cultivating Resilience and Adaptation for a Fulfilled Life

Resilience and adaptation are not innate traits but skills that can be cultivated and strengthened over time. By implementing the strategies outlined in this appendix, you can develop the tools needed to face life's challenges with confidence, flexibility, and grace. Whether inspired by the groundhog's quiet wisdom or your own inner strength, these practices will empower you to thrive in any environment and embrace the opportunities that change brings.

<u>Message from the Author:</u>

I hope you enjoyed this book, I love astrology and knew there was not a book such as this out on the shelf. I love metaphysical items as well. Please check out my other books:

-Life of Government Benefits

-My life of Hell

-My life with Hydrocephalus

-Red Sky

-World Domination:Woman's rule

-World Domination:Woman's Rule 2: The War

-Life and Banishment of Apophis: book 1

-The Kidney Friendly Diet

-The Ultimate Hemp Cookbook

-Creating a Dispensary(legally)

-Cleanliness throughout life: the importance of showering from childhood to adulthood.

-Strong Roots: The Risks of Overcoddling children

-Hemp Horoscopes: Cosmic Insights and Earthly Healing

- Celestial Hemp Navigating the Zodiac: Through the Green Cosmos

-Astrological Hemp: Aligning The Stars with Earth's Ancient Herb

-The Astrological Guide to Hemp: Stars, Signs, and Sacred Leaves

-Green Growth: Innovative Marketing Strategies for your Hemp Products and Dispensary

-Cosmic Cannabis

-Astrological Munchies

-Henry The Hemp

-Zodiacal Roots: The Astrological Soul Of Hemp

- Green Constellations: Intersection of Hemp and Zodiac

-Hemp in The Houses: An astrological Adventure Through The Cannabis Galaxy

-Galactic Ganja Guide

Heavenly Hemp

Zodiac Leaves

Doctor Who Astrology

Cannastrology

Stellar Satvias and Cosmic Indicas

Celestial Cannabis: A Zodiac Journey

AstroHerbology: The Sky and The Soil: Volume 1

AstroHerbology:Celestial Cannabis:Volume 2

Cosmic Cannabis Cultivation

The Starry Guide to Herbal Harmony: Volume 1

The Starry Guide to Herbal Harmony: Cannabis Universe: Volume 2

Yugioh Astrology: Astrological Guide to Deck, Duels and more

Nightmare Mansion: Echoes of The Abyss

Nightmare Mansion 2: Legacy of Shadows

Nightmare Mansion 3: Shadows of the Forgotten

Nightmare Mansion 4: Echoes of the Damned

The Life and Banishment of Apophis: Book 2

Nightmare Mansion: Halls of Despair

Healing with Herb: Cannabis and Hydrocephalus

Planetary Pot: Aligning with Astrological Herbs: Volume 1

Fast Track to Freedom: 30 Days to Financial Independence Using AI, Assets, and Agile Hustles

Cosmic Hemp Pathways

How to Become Financially Free in 30 Days: 10,000 Paths to Prosperity

Zodiacal Herbage: Astrological Insights: Volume 1

Nightmare Mansion: Whispers in the Walls

The Daleks Invade Atlantis

Henry the hemp and Hydrocephalus

10X The Kidney Friendly Diet
Cannabis Universe: Adult coloring book
Hemp Astrology: The Healing Power of the Stars
Zodiacal Herbage: Astrological Insights: Cannabis Universe: Volume 2
<u>Planetary Pot: Aligning with Astrological Herbs: Cannabis Universes: Volume 2</u>
Doctor Who Meets the Replicators and SG-1: The Ultimate Battle for Survival
Nightmare Mansion: Curse of the Blood Moon
<u>The Celestial Stoner: A Guide to the Zodiac</u>
Cosmic Pleasures: Sex Toy Astrology for Every Sign
Hydrocephalus Astrology: Navigating the Stars and Healing Waters
Lapis and the Mischievous Chocolate Bar

Celestial Positions: Sexual Astrology for Every Sign
Apophis's Shadow Work Journal: : A Journey of Self-Discovery and Healing
Kinky Cosmos: Sexual Kink Astrology for Every Sign
Digital Cosmos: The Astrological Digimon Compendium
Stellar Seeds: The Cosmic Guide to Growing with Astrology
Apophis's Daily Gratitude Journal

Cat Astrology: Feline Mysteries of the Cosmos
The Cosmic Kama Sutra: An Astrological Guide to Sexual Positions
Unleash Your Potential: A Guided Journal Powered by AI Insights
Whispers of the Enchanted Grove

Cosmic Pleasures: An Astrological Guide to Sexual Kinks

369, 12 Manifestation Journal

Whisper of the nocturne journal(blank journal for writing or drawing)

The Boogey Book

Locked In Reflection: A Chastity Journey Through Locktober

Generating Wealth Quickly:

How to Generate $100,000 in 24 Hours

Star Magic: Harness the Power of the Universe

The Flatulence Chronicles: A Fart Journal for Self-Discovery

The Doctor and The Death Moth

Seize the Day: A Personal Seizure Tracking Journal

The Ultimate Boogeyman Safari: A Journey into the Boogie World and Beyond

Whispers of Samhain: 1,000 Spells of Love, Luck, and Lunar Magic: Samhain Spell Book

Apophis's guides:

Witch's Spellbook Crafting Guide for Halloween

<u>Frost & Flame: The Enchanted Yule Grimoire of 1000 Winter Spells</u>

<u>The Ultimate Boogey Goo Guide & Spooky Activities for Halloween Fun</u>

Harmony of the Scales: A Libra's Spellcraft for Balance and Beauty

The Enchanted Advent: 36 Days of Christmas Wonders

Nightmare Mansion: The Labyrinth of Screams

Harvest of Enchantment: 1,000 Spells of Gratitude, Love, and Fortune for Thanksgiving

The Boogey Chronicles: A Journal of Nightly Encounters and Shadowy Secrets

The 12 Days of Financial Freedom: A Step-by-Step Christmas Countdown to Transform Your Finances

Sigil of the Eternal Spiral Blank Journal

A Christmas Feast: Timeless Recipes for Every Meal

Holiday Stress-Free Solutions: A Survival Guide to Thriving During the Festive Season

Yu-Gi-Oh! Holiday Gifting Mastery: The Ultimate Guide for Fans and Newcomers Alike

Holiday Harmony: A Hydrocephalus Survival Guide for the Festive Season

Celestial Craft: The Witch's Almanac for 2025 ‒ A Cosmic Guide to Manifestations, Moons, and Mystical Events

Doctor Who: The Toymaker's Winter Wonderland

Tulsa King Unveiled: A Thrilling Guide to Stallone's Mafia Masterpiece

Pendulum Craft: A Complete Guide to Crafting and Using Personalized Divination Tools

Nightmare Mansion: Santa's Eternal Eve

Starlight Noel: A Cosmic Journey through Christmas Mysteries

The Dark Architect: Unlocking the Blueprint of Existence

Surviving the Embrace: The Ultimate Guide to Encounters with The Hugging Molly

The Enchanted Codex: Secrets of the Craft for Witches, Wiccans, and Pagans

Harvest of Gratitude: A Complete Thanksgiving Guide

Yuletide Essentials: A Complete Guide to an Authentic and Magical Christmas

Celestial Smokes: A Cosmic Guide to Cigars and Astrology

Living in Balance: A Comprehensive Survival Guide to Thriving with Diabetes Insipidus

Cosmic Symbiosis: The Venom Zodiac Chronicles

The Cursed Paw of Ambition

Cosmic Symbiosis: The Astrological Venom Journal

Celestial Wonders Unfold: A Stargazer's Guide to the Cosmos (2024-2029)

The Ultimate Black Friday Prepper's Guide: Mastering Shopping Strategies and Savings

Cosmic Sales: The Astrological Guide to Black Friday Shopping

Legends of the Corn Mother and Other Harvest Myths

Whispers of the Harvest: The Corn Mother's Journal

The Evergreen Spellbook

The Doctor Meets the Boogeyman

The White Witch of Rose Hall's SpellBook

The Gingerbread Golem's Shadow: A Study in Sweet Darkness

The Gingerbread Golem Codex: An Academic Exploration of Sweet Myths

The Gingerbread Golem Grimoire: Sweet Magicks and Spells for the Festive Witch

The Curse of the Gingerbread Golem

10-minute Christmas Crafts for kids

<u>Christmas Crisis Solutions: The Ultimate Last-Minute Survival Guide</u>

Gingerbread Golem Recipes: Holiday Treats with a Magical Twist

The Infinite Key: Unlocking Mystical Secrets of the Ages

Enchanted Yule: A Wiccan and Pagan Guide to a Magical and Memorable Season

Dinosaurs of Power: Unlocking Ancient Magick

Astro-Dinos: The Cosmic Guide to Prehistoric Wisdom

Gallifrey's Yule Logs: A Festive Doctor Who Cookbook

The Dino Grimoire: Secrets of Prehistoric Magick

The Gift They Never Knew They Needed

The Gingerbread Golem's Culinary Alchemy: Enchanting Recipes for a Sweetly Dark Feast

A Time Lord Christmas: Holiday Adventures with the Doctor

Krampusproofing Your Home: Defensive Strategies for Yule

Silent Frights: A Collection of Christmas Creepypastas to Chill Your Bones

Santa Raptor's Jolly Carnage: A Dino-Claus Christmas Tale

If you want solar for your home go here: https://www.harborso-lar.live/apophisenterprises/

Get Some Tarot cards: https://www.makeplayingcards.com/sell/apophis-occult-shop

<u>Get some shirts: https://www.bonfire.com/store/apophis-shirt-emporium/</u>

<u>Instagrams:</u>
@apophis_enterprises,
@apophisbookemporium,
@apophisscardshop
Twitter: @apophisenterpr1
Tiktok:@apophisenterprise
Youtube: @sg1fan23477, @FiresideRetreatKingdom
Hive: @sg1fan23477
CheeLee: @SG1fan23477

Podcast: Apophis Chat Zone: https://open.spotify.com/show/ 5zXbrCLEV2xzCp8ybrfHsk?si=fb4d4fdbdce44dec

Newsletter: https://apophiss-newsletter-27c897.beehiiv.com/

If you want to support me or see posts of other projects that I have come over to: **buymeacoffee.com/mpetchinskg**
I post there daily several times a day

Get your Dinowicca or Christmas themed digital products, especially Santa Raptor songs and other musics. Here: **https://sg1fan23477.gumroad.com**

Apophis Yuletide Digital has not only digital Christmas items, but it will have all things with Dinowicca as well as other Digital products.